UNDENIABLE PRESENCE

An intimate and inspiring look at some of life's greatest challenges...and the hope that comes from God's undeniable presence

Heather H. Helton

Master of Divinity Candidate–Vanderbilt University

UNDENIABLE PRESENCE

Events in this book are based on Ms. Helton's recollection of real-life situations. However, the name of each patient discussed in this book has been changed. Additionally, in each medical case described, any identifying detail, such as patient's age, gender, ethnicity, occupation, familial relationships, place of residence, medical history, and/or diagnosis has been changed. Any resemblance to persons living or dead resulting from changes to names or other identifying details is purely coincidental and unintentional.

PHOTOGRAPHY, author photo: Jeremy Cowart

GRAPHIC DESIGN: McClearen Creative, Nashville, TN

ALL RIGHTS RESERVED
No part of this book may be reproduced without written permission of the publisher, except by a reviewer who wishes to quote brief passages.

Please direct inquires to:

Heather Helton:

www.heatherhhelton.com

Published by McClearen Creative, Nashville, TN

© 2018 Heather H. Helton

UNDENIABLE PRESENCE / **Heather H. Helton** —1st ed.

ISBN 978-1-7329228-0-8

DEDICATION

for Jude

    may your heart perpetually shine ~
    you are forever mommy's light

ACKNOWLEDGEMENTS

A sincere Thank You

~ to Jerry Crutchfield for believing these stories will bless others, and his unrelenting faith in me.

~ to Brenda McClearen for making this book come alive, and for her advice.

~ to Dimples Kellogg for her editing wisdom.

~ to all professors, current and past, who encouraged my creative writing.

~ to the patients who shared themselves, some through tears, some through laughs, but always through bravery.

~ to those who arise every day determined to make things better for others.

-CONTENTS-

Preface 7

Elizabeth – Retail Sales 9

Rita – Restaurant Server 11

Candace – Mom 15

Clark – Retired Repairman 17

Estelle – Family Matriarch 21

Flynn – Infant Boy 23

Betty – Church Secretary 25

The Reinhardt Family 29

Hailey – Kindergartner 31

Dan – Shop Owner 35

Emma – Nurse Assistant 37

Reilley – Teacher 41

Clara – Unemployed and Homeless 43

Jacob – Caretaker 45

Sylvia and Daniel – Wife and Son 49

Devon – House Painter 53

Maura – Mother and Baby Girl 55

Nadine – Pharmacist 57

Ted – Banker 61

Flora – Retired Bookkeeper 65

Meaghan – Mother 67

Marie – Mother 69

Carol – Real Estate Agent 73

Sarah – Retired Government Employee . . . 77

Malik – Store Manager 79

Tony – Unemployed 81

Lula – Retired Schoolteacher 85

John and Kathleen –
Media Consultant and Nurse 87

From the Author 89

Notes 90

PREFACE

Attending Vanderbilt Divinity School has been a life-changing event for me in so many ways that continue to reveal themselves on a daily basis. During my hospital internships, I have had the privilege and rare opportunity to interact with people from all walks of life and different races, creeds, and religions. All, however, faced life's ultimate battles for healing and survival. I'm truly grateful for these genuine and special real-life, real-time experiences.

When I think of an image of pastoral care, Jesus as shepherd immediately comes to mind. I see Him caring gently and lovingly for all God's creatures, great and small. I envision His all-encompassing love and care for each individual He encountered. It's then that I remember that His love and care are available to each of us if we so choose.

With this as my daily compass, I, as a chaplain, attempt to minister to others. While key traits include empathy, compassion, and tenderness, the key component for active and meaningful chaplaincy is presence. Quite simply put, that means to care enough to be there and listen while expressing the desire and willingness to provide comfort. We need not look any further than the stories of Jesus for lessons on how to be fully present for others. In John 10:11, Jesus said, "I am the good shepherd. The good shepherd lays down his life for the sheep." If we as chaplains, ministers, and stewards mirror this, the path is laid out before us.

Before I entered Vanderbilt Divinity School, which included Field Education and Clinical Pastoral Education, I had not encountered a lot of diversity within my social environment. Now, after engaging a great number of people as they faced serious illness or impending death, I learned that no matter where they fit within our social strata, the needs are the same. We all need love, compassion, and comfort, especially under life's most dire circumstances.

When I first began as chaplain during Clinical Pastoral Education at a small community hospital, and later, Field Education at a large urban hospital, I followed another chaplain for a preliminary period of about two weeks. I then had the opportunity to have my first solo visit. I felt prepared and enthusiastically looked forward to it.

As I began to have patient encounters, I realized that I had no idea about how intense and emotional they could be. Consequently, my initial response and overwhelming desire were to think in terms of how I might fix something...fix the illness, fix the despair and hopelessness of the patient and family member and even fix the future so this condition might never occur again. I soon learned after counselling with others, far more experienced than I, as well as from my own conclusions, that "fixing," was not my purpose and certainly not within my capabilities.

I soon learned that my most important role was to be present, listen, and attempt to bring comfort. In many cases as I began to face the inevitable and difficult questions such as, "Why me?" "Where is God?" "Tell me why?" and others, I developed a stronger sense of the reality that I just might not have the answers that people seek. But as I continued to try to be understanding and comforting, the questions sometimes seemed to answer themselves. Answered with the acknowledgment that God's love is abundant and available and surpasses all understanding. I became aware that I was comforted in these mutual encounters in a way that greatly strengthened my belief in God and the love of Jesus.

I'm pleased to share with you and blessed to be a part of some of the most amazing stories. Where is God? It became obvious and wonderfully comforting, that while not grammatically correct... "**I really don't know where God is not.**"

~ Heather H. Helton

Elizabeth, 52
Retail Sales

The room was filled to capacity with adults in sorrowful tears, some locking arms, some holding hands. This was Elizabeth's community of family, those who loved her most and loved her best. They hated to say good-bye to one who had been such an important and loving part of their lives, but sadly knew that her life on earth would soon be over. For reasons known only to God, it was Elizabeth's time.

The very air surrounding her bed seemed to waft a peaceful and calm feeling. The ventilator was preforming its life-maintaining job of keeping Elizabeth's lungs functioning in a labored manner. Her organs were in the process of shutting down. It was obviously a matter of very few minutes when I was paged to the ICU to see her family.

She had an angelic, sweet face, easily discernible even with the excessive tubing going into her mouth and nose. She looked at complete peace, her eyes slightly shuttered.

I held her right hand, stroking it softly, speaking to her in a low tone, "Elizabeth, your family is here. I am here. You are not alone. Most important, God is here with you right now."

One of the men asked if I would offer a prayer and pray aloud with them. I was truly humbled to be accepted so lovingly by this family during such a heartbreaking time. Knowing that this could be the last prayer delivered by anyone before she passed into eternity, I replied, "I would be honored to pray with you for her peace." They all stood, some quietly shuffling out of their chairs in an attempt to gather more closely. Hands were held as we formed a large circle of love around

Elizabeth's bed. I was right beside her head, focusing solely on her contented face. I knew this might be a most difficult prayer, but God led me and the words came.

"God, we come before You now, honoring You and in honor of the life of dear, precious Elizabeth. We thank You for her. She gave abundant love to her family for so many years. They are all gathered here in unity of love for her. We ask You to take her now where there will be no more suffering or pain, no more heartache, but only love and rejoicing in Your glorious Heaven. We ask that You usher healing into the hearts of her loved ones, giving them comfort and peace, knowing that Elizabeth will suffer no more. We thank you for the life of Elizabeth. We submit our prayers in the name of Jesus, our Lord and Savior. Amen."

At that point, we were all in tears. Elizabeth continued to rest peacefully, breathing her last breaths. The doctor then entered to remove the tubes. Everyone kissed her cheek or hand, stroked her hair, and bid her a final goodbye. Even in death, love wins...love of family without question, but faithfully the love of God who offers us peace and comfort in times of distress, unhappiness and even death.

> *"My Father's house has many rooms; if that were not so, would I have told you that I am going there to prepare a place for you? And if I go and prepare a place for you, I will come back and take you to be with me that you also may be where I am. You know the way to the place where I am going."*
> *~ John 14:2-4*
>
> *"On the death of a friend, we should consider that the fates through confidence have devolved on us the task of a double living, that we have henceforth to fulfill the promise of our friend's life also, in our own, to the world."*
> *~ Henry David Thoreau*

Rita, 67
Restaurant Server

When visiting with patients and their families in the hospital a chaplain tries to be prepared for the unexpected. Often, patients are not sure what the presence of a chaplain means. Some fear that possibly the chaplain is there after hearing of bad news regarding their health status. Consequently, they are hesitant to freely communicate until a bond of trust has been established. It's only then that the visit can become meaningful and comforting to the patient.

We all should be reminded that there are also those in need of love and comfort outside the walls of a hospital. And, here too, one never knows what to expect, especially in view of the fact that these encounters are totally unexpected.

In Massachusetts, my family and I were waiting for a table at a small coastal seafood restaurant. It was a picturesque scene, not fancy but colorfully resplendent with all the traditional seagoing artifacts and accoutrements to enhance the motif. As the host directed us to a table, I noticed a woman nearby with especially kind eyes, smiling sweetly at us. I nodded in acknowledgement, returning her smile. Her expression seemed to be sending a message that she had something to say. I often wonder if when our hearts and minds are open, we have a tendency to send vibes in ways that seem to offer others an invitation to speak out. I know that God has a way of creating special opportunities if we'll only be aware and receptive of His guidance.

She took a few steps to my side and said, "Hello, you look like someone I could talk to." Although somewhat taken aback, I immediately let her know I was more than willing to listen.

"I'm in a really bad way," she said. "Things have just ... things have just gotten too...hard," she painfully and hesitantly stated. The word *hard* rolled out of her mouth with much despair. She divulged that she worked fifty hours a week for minimum wage, had lost all contact with her adult children and grandchildren, lived alone, was widowed and depressed. The overcast gray sky from the windows behind her matched her sad demeanor. Rita truly felt all hope was lost at this point in her life. Her reaching out to me, a total stranger, was evidence of that.

I asked what I could do to help, immediately reminding myself that I had not chosen the best thing to say. The reality is I could do very little to help her situation. I could not get her family back, help her job situation, or find her another living environment. But I wanted to, so badly, and would have tried in any way possible. Quickly realizing the reality of my limitations, I looked directly into her eyes and said, "Rita, I'm here for you." After several more comments that woefully expressed other details of her life's circumstances, when finished, she seemed to be genuinely relieved as a smile returned to her face. God had put me in a situation where a person, lonely and facing overwhelming odds in her life, needed someone to listen and show care and concern. With her sweet smile now firmly etched back on her face, she thanked me for being there and letting her know that she mattered.

This was a first for me, providing chaplain/pastoral care service outside of a hospital setting. I was out "in the field" so to speak. A small dimly lit seafood restaurant overlooking the harbor was the last place I expected to respond as a chaplain ...more meaningfully, as someone who cares.

What I took with me that day remains indelibly strong in my mind. It expands and magnifies my awareness that there are people everywhere who want and need to be heard and feel that there are others who care. Ritas are everywhere. Ritas who seek comfort and need to know that others care enough to take the time to listen.

"Know this, my beloved brothers: let every person be quick to hear, slow to speak, slow to anger."
~ James 1:19

"When people talk, listen completely. Most people never listen."
~ Ernest Hemingway

Candace, 32
Mom

My first thought was, she's so young. Her head was bandaged all around, revealing only her bright blue eyes, nose, and mouth. I was seeing someone with a serious medical crisis, and I felt unsure about how to begin. Saying a silent prayer, I asked God to guide me. I said, "Hi, Candace," told her who I was, that I was a chaplain and would like to visit with her if she felt up to it at the moment. The corners of her parched lips turned slightly upward. "I have to apologize," she said in slurred words. "I got out of surgery just this morning and I'm still a little bit out of it." Considering her recent, and what appeared to be a major surgical procedure, I thought she was looking and acting extraordinarily well. She was alert and even a bit chipper. "I had a brain tumor taken out," she said. I commented how well it appeared she was doing and asked how she was feeling in other ways, wondering about her other concerns and worries.

As she adjusted herself in the bed, I could see that she was clutching a photo of three young children. She glanced down and pointed them out to me. With an expression of complete love and devotion, she said, "These are my loves, Alex, Ava, and Audrey. I can't leave them," she said as tears began to glisten in her deep blue eyes. "I have to get better and get out of here." Her words were weighted with longing and hopeful determination. I reached for her hand.

She was very open and honest in expressing her deepest feelings. Candace began to speak about her faith, starting in childhood. She'd grown up as a Methodist, sung in church every Sunday, and was now heavily involved in her church community. She was a young woman who believed strongly in God and had been faithful in her belief and commitment to Him.

Her mom and grandmother then came in with coffees in hand. As I introduced myself, Candace asked, "Will you lead a prayer please?" The tone of her voice and the look on her face let me know that prayer was a vital and meaningful part of her life. The others set their coffees down on her hospital tray and in a moment of silent unity, the hands of all four women reached out to one another. An unannounced but mutual expression of faith was exhibited and felt in the holding of hands. At once it felt holy as we invited God's spirit into our midst. I began by thanking God for the success of Candace's surgery, then prayed for her full healing. The women echoed with solemn "amens" after each refrain. Prayers were then raised for her precious three children who so much needed their mother to return home.

Without question Candace's faith was the catalyst and center of this petition before God.

"For where two or three have gathered together in My name, I am there in their midst."
~ Matthew 18:20

"Joy is prayer; joy is strength: joy is love; joy is a net of love by which you can catch souls."
~ Mother Teresa

Clark, 81
Retired Repairman

Alzheimer's is the thief of life that continues taking until there's nothing left to take. The painful experience of watching a family member succumb to this dreadful disease, little by little, bit by bit, day by day, then finally disappearing until there's no one left is heart wrenching and devastating. A horrific and unwanted chapter of life, it is extremely hurtful to witness someone who has been a loving family member and who has provided comfort and companionship for a great number of years experience total deterioration.

I met Clark when he was completely in the throes of this terrible disease, deteriorating slowly and surely. I was very pleased that we had a series of positive encounters. These pleasant experiences tend to give hope for improvement or at least a slowdown in symptoms.

On this particular Tuesday as I went to spend time with Clark, I expected the same as before. But a major characteristic of Alzheimer's is unpredictability. I walked in, enthusiastic and excited to see him. He had asked to see me because he had a question. Considering the times we'd spent together in previous visits, I saw this as a good sign. I assumed I had gained his trust and found this comforting and fulfilling.

I entered his room then took the usual side chair to his bedside, ready to hear his thoughts and questions. Immediately, I could tell something had drastically changed with him, however. He was furious with me. His face was frightening to look at. I smiled cautiously but sincerely and asked him what he wanted to ask me. "Why did you steal all my money? I trusted you!" he exclaimed loudly and intensely. His booming voice echoed down the hospital hall.

At once I felt humiliated and scared, but also felt sadness for Clark. Seeing this sudden, dramatic shift into total paranoia was very difficult to handle. My mixed emotions ran from fright and sorrow to complete inadequacy. He had been such a kind and gentle man, and I wanted to believe that somehow he would be again soon.

As I sat stunned beyond belief, he continued his tirade, "You stole from me! I confided in you and told you everything! You took everything I own out of this room!" In an effort that took everything I could muster, I calmly assured him that I had not done what he claimed. I reminded him who I was and calmly explained that I wanted to be his friend and always looked forward to visiting with him. He then added that I had risked his entire family's lives in an intentional fire. As preposterous as this accusation was, I attempted to reassure him that this wasn't true.

I cared deeply for Clark and felt that somehow our visits had been meaningful and helpful. I was broken and heart sick that our chaplain-patient relationship that I had nurtured and felt so good about had suffered such a destructive blow by the evil hand of Alzheimer's. But I also understood. Clark was being taken on a ride not of his own choosing.

In ensuing conversations with family members of other Alzheimer's victims, I found that most seek a variety of methods and endeavors for help, strength, and guidance. Many read and research diligently the latest available information, always with the hope of a new and helpful breakthrough. Others have said that while dealing with the pain and agony of this horrible life experience, they find surrounding themselves with soothing music is comforting and consoling. And there are other methods as well.

But one, the most important of all, never failing and most often quoted is, "You will need God."

"The light shines in the darkness, and the darkness has not overcome it."
~ John 1:5

"In order for the light to shine so brightly, the darkness must be present."
~ Francis Bacon

Estelle, 99
Family Matriarch

Upon being admitted to the hospital, Estelle had asked to see a chaplain. She had several health issues including emphysema, depression, renal failure, and heart disease. She was aware that her time on this earth was limited. Unsure about what state I might find her in, I was intrigued to be visiting a near-centenarian.

She was sleeping, a blue and yellow hand-woven blanket tucked neatly under her chin. I didn't want to disturb her sound rest and quietly turned to exit. As I took a few steps, she said, "Hello! Who are you?" I approached her bedside, showed her my ID, and explained that I was the chaplain and had come to visit her. "Oh good!" she replied. "I've been waiting to see you."

I discovered a padded chair against the wall and moved it closer to be at her side."How are you feeling today, Estelle?" I asked.

She exhaled as if a lot of information was forthcoming. Her frail fingers reached over for my hand. "I'm not well, dear. Not well at all. But you know, I've had a really good long life. I have my children and grandchildren and great-grandchildren ...friends, church, and a strong faith in God. I have all I need." Estelle's voice shook with age and weakness, but her hand was strong, grasping mine. I smiled, and before I could reply, with a look of understanding that conveyed many well learned lessons of life, she said intently, "Enjoy the time you have." I smiled, so very thankful, while realizing the availability of the many blessings of a loving God.

Estelle's words, which I took with me from that day, still ring loud and clear: "I have all I need." More than ever it became abundantly clear that Estelle's formula for fulfillment in life is a lesson for us all.

> *"So we do not lose heart. Even though our outer nature is wasting away, our inner nature is being renewed day by day."*
> *~ II Corinthians 4:16*

> *"Even in the mud and scum of things, something always, always sings."*
> *~ Ralph Waldo Emerson*

Flynn, 11 Days Old
Infant Boy

Flynn emerged into this world in a troubling and heart-wrenching manner. Little Flynn was born addicted to a drug. His condition was resoundingly better than it had been upon his arrival into this world eleven days ago. His body was no longer prone to shuddering, his color a translucent pale pink, and his cries were diminished.

His mother was understandably weepy and forlorn. As I listened intently to her story, I was surprised. Before her pregnancy with Flynn, she became dependent on a painkiller after several surgeries. However, upon discovering she was pregnant, she stopped cold turkey. The doctor then prescribed a different medicine to counter the effects of the first. Thus, she had tried to do the best for her baby. Despite the difficult beginning, Flynn, who was loved and being cared for, seemed to be gaining by the hour. With my hand on his bright red hair, I prayed aloud for God to increase his strength, his ability to overcome obstacles he wasn't yet old enough to understand, all with the hope that he had a future of potential good health and happiness. As those tiny pink C-shaped ears heard the blessings being prayed for in his behalf, I asked that God would bestow His healing power upon Flynn.

As I gently touched his fragile head, prayers were quietly spoken, calling upon a loving and merciful God to send forth healing for Flynn.

> *"He called a child, whom he put among them, and said, 'Truly I tell you, unless you change and become like children, you will never enter the kingdom of heaven. Whoever becomes humble like this child is the greatest in the kingdom of heaven. Whoever welcomes one such child in my name welcomes me.'"*
> *~ Matthew 18:2-5*

> *"Listen to the mustn'ts, child. Listen to the don'ts. Listen to the shouldn'ts, the impossibles, the won'ts. Listen to the never haves, then listen close to me...Anything can happen, child. Anything can be."*
> *~ Shel Silverstein*

Betty, 50
Church Secretary

The beeper announced an emergency page. A trauma situation was developing in the ER and possibly a chaplain was needed. Entering these unknown and tragic scenes was a bit frightening for me as a young chaplain on my first internship. There is no way of knowing what the circumstances might be or what could be just around the corner. But it's imperative and required to muster up the confidence and courage to face whatever I might encounter for the patient, and the family.

As I entered the ER, doing my best to be prepared for this emergency, I uttered a prayer that God would give me strength to be adequate in my role as a chaplain, and to bless and watch over those involved in this tragic occurrence. I asked the nurse at the front desk about the situation. At that same moment, I saw a gurney hurriedly wheeled in from the rear door in the ambulance area. A paramedic was atop the patient and administering CPR. A swarm of people surrounded the gurney rushing into the trauma bay. I stood back, unsure of my place in this frantic moment. I didn't want to go in while immediate medical attention was needed. I was looking around for family members, but didn't see anyone with the patient at the moment other than staff.

At once I saw definite evidence of blood on his shoes. I asked the head nurse what happened. She said the young man had been struck by a car while walking. The day had been a beautiful one, not a cloud in the sky. He had gone out for a leisurely walk and never came home. And now, here he was in severe trauma, and no doubt, his family in near hysterics. The nurse agreed that I should stand aside until all available medical assistance was given him, and until I was appropriately needed.

While I was waiting, I turned to see a woman sitting on a gurney beside me. She had a warm, genuine smile and immediately extended her hand. "Hi, I'm Betty," she said kindly.

"Hi there, Betty." Then I told her who I was.

Betty said, "Oh! You're a chaplain? Well, I'd like to talk to you...bad scene going on in there isn't it?"

I replied, "Yes, it is," as I paused to look back into the trauma bay. Turning my attention back to her, I asked, "Betty, what brings you to the hospital?"

"Can't you tell?" she said with a laugh as she looked down. I followed her gaze and instantly realized that she had no legs extending below her gown. "I lost my legs from the knees down when I was a little girl. But I'm here because I think I have pneumonia," she replied, coughing persistently, while smiling at her own joke about her legs. She coughed again, somewhat violently, and said, "even though I didn't have legs growing up, and depended on a wheelchair to get around, I'm okay. I'm not mad at God. These things happen to people all over the place all the time."

Betty's solid expression of faith and acceptance of her tremendous personal loss was a testimony that spoke volumes. I was reminded of what I had been discovering more and more in my role as chaplain. While, with my greatest desire and best intentions to help and comfort others, I continued to be helped and comforted and richly blessed by others like Betty.

With a tone of self-assuredness, Betty looked at me and said, "Well, chaplain...we do all we can do," and then pointing upward, she said, "the rest we just leave to the Big Guy."

One might think that Betty's expression was a bit cavalier, but the tone of her voice and the expression on her face left no doubt of her strong belief in God and the power of prayer.

Many times, God's blessing comes from unexpected directions. I was there with a family who was experiencing the dreaded anxiety of waiting for news of a loved one...while hoping and praying that the news would be good. Then, along comes Betty with her precious smile, endearing flippant comment, and good-natured manner, wanting to tell how God had richly blessed her despite the life-altering loss of both legs. It was a rare and inspiring experience to be etched forever in my memory.

After a period of waiting, hoping, and praying, the trauma patient revived, and I had the chance to visit him briefly. He would need multiple surgeries and long rehab, but the odds were in his favor.

Betty waved as I walked out of the trauma bay. "Thank you, Betty. You were a gift today," I nearly shouted.

"You're the chaplain who knows the Big Guy!" she said with a laugh. "I'm just a woman with no legs," and she laughed again. I looked into her deep blue eyes and said, "No Ma'am. You are Betty, and you are powerful and strong with a beautiful belief in God that is a blessing to others." With a slight smile, I looked at her and said, "Obviously, you know the Big Guy, too."

"I am confident of this, that the one who began a good work among you will bring it to completion by the day of Jesus Christ."
~ Philippians 1:6

"Only in the darkness can you see the stars."
~ Martin Luther King Jr.

The Reinhardt Family

Walking past the gurneys in the hallway, I rushed into the small private family room in the emergency area. Dimly lit, it was furnished with simple chairs, nondescript artwork, and random boxes of tissues. I had been paged for an emergency room visit with a family and braced myself for the worst. Not too long ago I had been in this same scenario with my own family, anxiously biding time in an ER waiting room.

I thought I was prepared as a chaplain to handle the dynamics of an emergency room crisis, but standing in similar shoes is not the "same" shoes.

I entered to find the room filled with people weeping and murmuring in low tones. A heavy cloud of hurt hovered over them. I sat in the only available chair next to a woman who looked at me tearfully in anguish and pain. She said, "She was here just today, having lunch with us." The woman continued to cry. "Then she was gone. It makes no sense."

The woman across from her stated, "Sis, she was ninety-five. It was her time." The first woman, obviously perturbed, shouted out, "Have some compassion! She was here this morning, and now she's gone! Look at her grandkids here! Can you just show some empathy and understanding?"

Others in the room and I were surprised by this heated exchange, but then I remembered in the middle of this verbal storm that everyone grieves differently. One daughter was despairing in tears and tissues, while the other was in total acceptance and was now exploring her phone.

I placed my hand on the sobbing daughter, hoping to provide caring consolation. From the bottom of my heart I became aware that I was not at all sure about what was appropriate to say. I felt uncomfortable and couldn't locate the suitable words in my brain to say. I felt inept. When I found myself in an ER family room four years earlier, I was not so speechless. I was begging for information, hoping and praying for a different outcome. After that personal experience, I told myself that maybe now this would be a type of visit I could better handle. But, here it was, and I wasn't as prepared as I had hoped.

I now felt that my presence was required to at least initiate a dialogue that would enable and encourage family members to interact with love and understanding, express their deepest feelings, and recall happy memories and shared times from the past. Although I wanted so badly to have meaningful things to say, things lofty and inspiring to bring comfort and to help them in their time of grief, I was aware that I had come up short and felt I had let them down. Then I remembered the age-old hymn, "Take It To the Lord in Prayer," which leads to the ultimate path for those who trust and believe in the healing power and love of God.

We prayed together, asking for peace within their hearts and peace for their mother.

"So now faith, hope, and love abide, these three; but the greatest of these is love."
~ 1 Corinthians 13:13

"I've learned that people will forget what you said, people will forget what you did, but people will never forget how you made them feel."
~ Maya Angelou

Hailey, 5
Kindergartner

Her golden blonde hair was splayed on her pillow like expanding rays from the sun. But her shining and infectious grin offered the brightest light. She wasn't worried about a thing. Little Hailey had five My Little Pony plush dolls surrounding her. She was performing a play with them positioned on her tummy when I walked in. "So, you need to fly to school, go to class, then fly home after school," she was saying with the toys, two held lovingly in her little hands. "Okay, Mommy Pony, I'll see you soon!" Hailey was deep into her activity, so much so that my entrance didn't seem to faze her. Her left hand was bruised and taped down with an inserted IV that looked much too large for such a little girl. Her fingernails were painted a bright aqua blue. She was happily and completely lost in her world of make-believe. I hesitated to walk in for fear that I might interrupt her play.

For a few moments, I sat quietly near the door, observing her and her exceptional, wondrous child demeanor. The nurse had told me her parents stepped out to talk with the doctor. It was just the two of us, strangers about to meet. I was unsure of her complete diagnosis, but the nurse explained Hailey had been hospitalized a great deal lately.

She looked over at me as she snuggled her ponies. "Who are you?" her sweet voice inquired.

"Hi, Hailey! I'm Heather, and I wanted to say hi and visit with you," I replied.

"What do you do?" she asked.

"Well, I visit patients in the hospital and check in on them and their families. I also love to listen to people," I tried to explain. I figured uttering the term "chaplain" would not do much to convey why I had come to see her.

"So you listen? That's your job?" she asked.

"Actually, it is, Hailey. That's exactly what I do." Hailey seemed pleased. She introduced me to Becky, Lily, Maddie, Claire, and Ella, her ponies. I recalled from childhood loving stuffed animals and dolls and could readily imagine the comfort and joy they brought to her. We talked more about her ponies and shared our love for animals.

Then, out of the blue, she said, "It's my tummy...that's what's wrong." I was attempting to stay upbeat and fun in our conversation, but I wanted to give her a chance to express any concerns and worries she might have. "I have a sick tummy, that's all," she grimaced with a cute expression as she touched her abdomen.

"Hailey, I'm so sorry to hear about your sick tummy," I responded. "And I hope it gets all better very soon."

Just then, her parents entered the room, looking somewhat surprised to see me. I was explaining to them who I was when Hailey shouted, "She's a listener. She listens!"

In the precious short time that I had been with her, every ounce of love and compassion within me had responded, endearing this beautiful child to me. Her parents were very receptive to my presence and within minutes asked me to pray for Hailey. She was about to go for her first scan to determine her prognosis. Her parents were obviously concerned and worried about the outcome, but their strong faith was also apparent. As I moved closer to her, almost instantly, Hailey stuck out her hand for me to hold, IV and all. I laid out my palm so she could rest her hand in mine. Her parents hugged each other, her mother touching her foot as I prayed aloud for Hailey's healing. At the conclusion of the prayer, Hailey followed with a confident and loud "A-men!"

Her response let me know that even at the age of five, Hailey had an awareness of God and was familiar with going to Him in prayer.

Witnessing children in pain is perhaps the most difficult aspect of spending time with patients. But Hailey's sunny disposition helped everyone stay upbeat and positive in her presence. Although seriously ill, she exhibited optimism and boundless joy and exuded a peace that possibly only little children know. No doubt, Hailey is one of God's greatest gifts.

"Jesus said, 'Let the little children come to me, and do not stop them; for it is to such as these that the kingdom of heaven belongs.'"
~ Matthew 19:14

"Happiness can be found even in the darkest times if one only remembers to turn on the light."
~ J.K. Rowling, Harry Potter

Dan, 86
Shop Owner

Dan was a weekly day client at a memory loss facility. He was fairly reclusive, but on occasion he could be coaxed out of his shell. On our first visit, he was full-on turtle. I really tried, however gently, to get to know him, but it wasn't time. And that was okay. This was on Dan's terms, not mine, and that's the way it has to go. Dan was ex-military and struggled immensely with the fact he had killed people. I know because he told me every day at least four times a day. He carried a submarine's weight of guilt in his marrow for the deaths he caused. This was my first encounter with a patient enduring this kind of heartbreaking, ongoing guilt and shame.

On our second visit, I began to see more of the real Dan. He carried around a stack of books and had just set them down. I asked if I might have a look, and he obliged. His watercolors were spectacular! It was hard to believe these gorgeous images were concealed from the world. He shyly downplayed his artistry when I complimented his work.

We kept conversation light and in his comfort zone until the war memories suddenly shot through him like a bullet. He felt that he just had to tell me. He felt like a horrible human being for having killed people in war. He described it to me in grave, gory detail...his finger on the trigger, the sound, the blood, the fall, all of it. He wept. He wept every time for three months. His palpable pain was his constant companion.

What could I provide an emotionally wounded veteran with dementia? I struggled to find answers about how to truly help him. I soon realized I might be the only person with whom he felt comfortable enough to share his story. So I listened. I listened and learned much about Dan.

After many visits, he seemed to become more willing to communicate with a newfound calmness. Through much prayer and meditation, we sought peace and comfort for him, making progress while fully knowing that the power of God surpasses all.

"Not only that, but we also boast in our sufferings, knowing that suffering produces endurance, and endurance produces character, and character produces hope."
~ Romans 5:3-4

"We must be willing to let go of the life we've planned, so as to have the life that is waiting for us."
~ Joseph Campbell

Emma, 22
Nurse Assistant

It was an urgent page, a Code Red. The staff went into emergency mode and attempted to assess the situation and act accordingly. The only information available at that time was coming loud and clear over the speaker system with the dire announcement of "potential shooter" within the hospital. I was in the Pastoral Care area and was unsure about whether to run, hide, shut the door, or flee. Fortunately, this community hospital had an established procedure in place for such an event. The patients' doors automatically close and lock when there is a Code Red. But for interns and staff, as well as for me, the appropriate procedure in this very serious and panicky situation was not clear.

After staying put for a few minutes in the office, I decided to peek around the hallway. I saw no one. All was eerily quiet. As I returned to the office, I saw someone leaning against a window, sobbing heavily. Immediately sensing that there was a problem, I called out, "Are you okay?" There was no answer. Just then the speaker announced that the Code Red was cancelled. I ran back to check on the person who was distraught. She was near collapse. We were the only ones in the area. I put my arms around her, holding her as I sought to offer comfort. She seemed to be in uncontrollable pain. She tried to talk, but her words were incomprehensible. Her small frame shook in my arms. "I'm sorry, I'm so sorry," she said. "I'm so scared," she cried. "I just got out of nursing school. This is my first week at my first job, and already, there's a possible shooter!"

Emma was terrified. I held her, continuing to try to calm her and provide comfort. She began to speak about her fear of the reality that shootings can happen anytime, anywhere. She had worked so hard to get through school, had secured this wonderful first job, and now, with no warning, was faced with a possible life-or-death situation. It was too much.

I suggested that she ask her supervisor if she might go home awhile to regain her composure and regroup after such an upsetting event. She was young and wide-eyed but revealed that she was fully dedicated to fulfilling her commitment of helping and caring for others. The last thing she expected, however, was to be in the immediate proximity of a potential deadly situation that involved a shooter.

I tried to assure Emma that few people, if any, would react any differently to such threatening circumstances, and that no special heroic actions were called for. She appeared to relax and be a bit more in control. It occurred to me that as honorable as her choice to become a nurse had been, with all the more normal things she had trained for and expected to encounter, life is so uncertain in so many ways. It's impossible to be prepared for everything that might come her way.

It also occurred to me that the only way we can be prepared for the unexpected is to feel that God is with us, will look after us and give us comfort, grace, and peace.

With that in mind and in that moment, all I could do was try to be there for her. In the future, I'm sure she will be there for others.

"Who is going to harm you if you are eager to do good? But even if you should suffer for what is right, you are blessed. "Do not fear their threats; do not be frightened.'"
~ I Peter 3:13-14

"You gain strength, courage, and confidence by every experience in which you really stop to look fear in the face. You are able to say to yourself, 'I lived through this horror. I can take the next thing that comes along.'"
~ Eleanor Roosevelt

Reilley, 32
Teacher

On the first day of my internship, I entered a room in the palliative care unit. This is akin to hospice in that the patients are entering the season of finality of life, however, with the utmost care, compassion, and pain management. Reilley was leaning over, hands folded on his mother's bed, his face filled with countless memories and compassion. She was resting, peacefully awaiting the next and last phase of her earthly presence. Her paper-thin eyelids were delicately closed. She was not in pain, but Reilley clearly was. One knows when the machines are no longer present, the hour is drawing near. No needle, IV, or life support was anywhere in sight.

"I came to see if I could visit with you and your mom," I quietly said. He looked at her lovingly, then looked back at me. His eyes reflected a lifetime of love and adoration. "Miss," he said, "honestly I thank you for coming, but we asked for a Catholic priest." When a family and/or patient enters a hospital, they can request specific faith background for visits. For some reason, the paperwork was in error. They did not want to see an interfaith chaplain. I understood completely. I had worked at a primarily Catholic hospital in the past and knew full well that when one is expected to pass soon, the family wants the last rites that must be given by a priest.

I apologized to Reilley for the mixup, promising to contact the priest on call. As I turned to leave, however, he stopped me with a question. "Before you go, may I ask you to pray for my mom? Her name is Evelyn. She raised seven of us on her own after dad left. She literally worked her entire life. Even though I can see she's now in a peaceful place, it still hurts so bad...it hurts to let her go." I went to his mother's bedside, immediately thankful for his willingness to request prayer for her.

I wasn't the spiritual care person they requested, but my inner prayer now was that maybe I could be of some help and that my presence in some way could be meaningful and comforting.

As I began to offer up my prayer for Evelyn, I was strongly reminded that whether Catholic, Protestant, or other persuasions of faith, our God is a loving God, and He is faithful to those who believe and seek Him. Prayer is the key to Heaven. Faith unlocks the door.

I spoke words for Evelyn and also words for Reilley. I fervently prayed for peace and comfort for both of them and felt strongly that God was present in that room.

> *"...with all humility and gentleness, with patience, bearing with one another in love, & making every effort to maintain the unity of the Spirit in the bond of peace."*
> *~ Ephesians 4:2-3*
>
> *"If we have no peace, it is because we have forgotten that we belong to each other."*
> *~ Mother Teresa*

Clara, 68
Unemployed, Homeless

Clara was suffering from double pneumonia and schizophrenia. At the foot of her bed was a large tan dog, panting and almost seeming to smile. She pointed and said to me, "That's Ralphie...my only friend." Ralphie was wearing a vest indicating that he was an emotional support pet. It was a bit surprising to see this giant animal within hospital walls. Clara then said that most people seem to care only for her dog and not for her. I assured her that while I liked Ralphie a lot, I was there just for her. Upon hearing this, she collapsed in tears.

Clara had not a single penny to her name. In honest and somewhat frightening details, she described her living situation that revealed she lived in a tent by a river about twenty miles away. She was very ill, intermittently coughing and wheezing, her body shaking violently. She stated that she got double pneumonia because her tent "had holes in it from the rats."

My eyes began to fill with tears as she continued to tell me about the condition and details of her existence. "When I get out of here, I got nowhere to go...got no money and no one." She began to cry and leaned over to hug Ralphie for comfort. I had such an overwhelming desire to say, "I'll help you find housing, food, employment, and money," although knowing that my immediate and authorized purpose to be there was to listen and offer what comfort and support I was capable of giving.

She briefly stopped crying, then said, "I don't know much, but I know God is with me...all the time." What an astounding revelation to come from her! Clara was seriously ill, had nothing but a dog and a tent filled with holes, but a mountain-strong faith that under the most trying circumstances kept her going.

In her overwhelming condition of life, Clara still found solace and the will to go on by believing that "God is with me... all the time." What an incredible commentary and testimony for us all.

> *"Do not be afraid—I am with you! I am your God—let nothing terrify you! I will make you strong and help you; I will protect you and save you."*
> *~ Isaiah 41:10*
>
> *"There is a crack in everything. That's how the light gets in."*
> *~ Leonard Cohen*

Jacob, 23
Caretaker

Jacob was a young man who looked vital, normal, and healthy. Many times, however, serious medical issues cannot be diagnosed or even recognized, based on appearance. Jacob had acquired a treacherous and quite serious infection that was due to ongoing health problems that had spanned his young life. In addition to his own health crisis, which could not be taken lightly, there was another issue affecting him negatively. It was an issue of major concern to him, and he regarded his illness secondary to it.

Jacob was the primary caretaker for his mom, who was suffering with ALS. His dad had long left the scene. Jacob's assistance was vital for all of her basic needs, including bathing and feeding among other functions of responsibility. In a way their roles were now reversed. From the time he was born, his mother had parented and cared for him in all the ways a loving parent would. From the basic needs of food and shelter, she had loved, comforted, and encouraged him. Now, he was more than willing to do the same for her. Even though a temporary nurse was presently caring for her, being in the hospital and away from her caused him much anxiety and pain. Jacob knew she needed him back as soon as possible, and he found it difficult to suppress the anguish he was feeling, especially since he knew that her condition was rapidly deteriorating.

He welcomed me into his room with a wonderful and optimistic smile, not looking at all like you would expect someone with his condition to look. Had it not been for an IV pumping fluids into his arm, one might believe he was just lying there taking a short nap. After a few minutes of introduction and becoming comfortable with each other, he began to tell about his current medical condition and relayed all of the information he had regarding his health crisis. It soon became obvious, however, that his mom's health and the difficulties she faced were his most urgent concern. "I have got to get back to Momma," he said with an overwhelming look of compassion on his face. "No one can or will do for her everything she needs. She needs me, and as long as I can do it, I intend to take care of her." Such love and commitment expressed by a son for his mother were very special to witness.

Even with Jacob's debilitating condition, his focus was centered on getting out of the hospital as soon as possible and returning to assist his mother. Then, in a somewhat faltering voice, he looked at me and said, "I have a problem I could use your help with." As chaplains, we can't do anything by way of medical assisting, but I was bracing for anything he might request. It was always difficult to say no to patients, but often we are required to when it is beyond the bounds of responsibility. And so I listened.

"They give me this one pill. They say it will help to take the infection away," he said. "But"...he stalled while turning to look at the medicine bottle. "It makes me so nauseous. Then they have to give me something to stop the nausea. I've decided I'm not going to take it anymore. What do you think?"

Suddenly, I found myself in what was a potential crisis. I knew not to interfere with anyone's medical protocol but didn't want to abandon the progress our communication had made, and the comfort level we had established.

He asked again, "Well, do you think I should stop taking it? Don't you think God can heal me without taking it?" Oh boy, I thought. Now I'm in even deeper waters. We've gone from his wanting medical advice to telling him what I think God thinks.

"Jacob," I said, "I believe God provides doctors and medical facilities to help us in times of physical needs, and proper medications to treat those needs. I think you want to get healed and get out of here without having to come back."

He looked at me with total understanding and said, "No...I don't want to have to ever, ever come back here."

At that point, he seemed to be regaining a sense of reality. After a brief hesitation, he fumbled on the side table until he found it ... then opened the bottle. "You're right," he said. "I can deal with the nausea, and my Momma needs me."

I was strongly and faithfully reminded of the biblical passage that says, "the greatest of these is love."

"Lord Almighty, blessed is the one who trusts in you."
~ Psalm 84:12

"The best way to find out if you can trust somebody is to trust them."
~ Ernest Hemingway

Sylvia and Daniel, 64 & 32
Wife and Son

A quiet, reverent chapel occupies a small area in most hospitals. Typically, you will find in it literature related to various faiths and denominations, including pamphlets, books, and Bibles. This is available for patients and families who seek solitude and meditation during medical crises. Often, brief weekly or biweekly series of consultations occur in this special space. Additionally, prayer boxes may be available so that the names of those in need may be lifted up by chaplains, ministers, or priests. The chapel is a solemn place of restoration meant for private reflections, thoughts, and prayers.

On this particular afternoon, I was surprised to overhear sad wailing and moaning as I passed by the chapel door. I turned to lean my head in and observed a small woman leaning over the chairs, her body rocking gently in a slow and anguished motion. A man to her right appeared to be looking out the stain glass window nearby. At first, I hesitated at the door as I was unsure of the situation and didn't want to intrude inappropriately. Should I wait and allow them their privacy to deal with their circumstances, or should I proceed to explore the possibility that I might be helpful in some way? While I was aware that they might be receptive to my entering as a chaplain, I also knew that the opposite could be true. In an intense time, a stranger entering their midst might be an intrusion.

Reminding myself of the commitment I had made to try to bring comfort and help to others, after a moment of deliberation, I walked in and tried to assess the situation as quickly as possible. The woman I had spied earlier leaned over and reached out her hand. I hurried to her side, kneeling at her winter boots. I began to tell her who I was and why I was there. She said her name was Sylvia, and then cried out, "We have a big problem here."

"Mom," the man next to her responded, "We don't know what Dad wants." She looked at him in total disappointment as he made his way to the chair beside her. I immediately wondered, then asked if I might help in any way. Sylvia said, "It's my husband, Jack. He was in an accident and he's now in a coma. They don't"...she stopped to breathe and wipe a tear ..."don't know for sure if he'll make it or not. And he always made me promise, no life support." The son immediately spoke up, "But, Mom, there's a chance he will recover. We have to take that chance."

While I was still kneeling and holding her hand, she and her son began whispering back and forth, each expressing thoughts and feelings about the best course of action to be taken for Jack, the husband and father. Although it was not the choice she preferred, Sylvia was feeling the pressure of a conflicting promise she'd made to Jack.

I prayed that they could resolve this in love and consideration for each other, leading them to the wisest decision for Jack. Here was a situation of differing opinions, both steeped in love and concern that they hoped would lead to the best decision.

Family dynamics can be complicated, emotion filled, while being both logical and illogical...especially in times of health crises. For some families these circumstances have been addressed and dealt with from a legal standpoint, leaving nothing to chance. Other times, as in this case, it's an exhaustive decision to be made by loving family members as they strive to do their best. Jack's wife, Sylvia, and his son, Daniel, loved him and each other enough to exhaust all efforts to obtain the best for Jack, and to genuinely listen to each other.

After much more heartfelt communication and prayer, a decision was finally made to continue with life support. It doesn't always go this way, but Jack later made a full recovery.

"Let us hold fast the confession of our hope without wavering, for He who promised is faithful."
~ Hebrews 10:23

"You don't choose your family. They are God's gift to you, as you are to them."
~ Desmond Tutu

Devon, 30
House Painter

Devon, a young man of thirty, was a house painter who immigrated to the United States. He had been in this country just two months when he was in a horrific truck accident. Fire consumed him to the point of near death. Burned over 75 percent of his body, he was covered in blue sheets from neck to feet. He struggled to speak in a warbled fashion as best he could with intense and debilitating pain coursing through him. He could barely manage to get out so much as a single lucid word. As I looked at him, I wondered what someone in such overwhelming pain would find necessary to try to say. Five nurses attempted to find a vein, any vein that was receptive and usable for an IV. The bright yellow lamp lights seemed to burn into the sheets, bathing him with unwanted heat. Devon was in the throes of life-and-death pain.

Still, he kept trying to form words with his chafed lips, so obviously prominent, swollen, and painful on his badly burned face. As his chaplain, I felt the instinct and inclination to touch his shoulder in a reassuring manner but realized that this could only provide additional torment. He began trying to speak. I leaned in close to try to hear the words and understand him. With steady eyes and in a hesitant manner, Devon said, "We are all equal in the eyes of God." What! Did I hear and understand him correctly? My immediate thoughts and feelings humbled and renewed me. While I was attempting to be caring, comforting, and supportive to someone who was at the point of death, suffering unbearable pain, he was assuring me that we are all equal in the eyes of God.

Due to his labored and slurred speech, I can't be sure of what all Devon was communicating in that moment, but it was obvious that he had peace and understanding that come only from an abiding faith in a loving God.

With thankful awareness, I realized that there are countless lessons to be learned in our attempts to help others.

> *"There is neither Jew nor Gentile, neither slave nor free, nor is there male and female, for you are all one in Christ Jesus."*
> *~ Galatians 3:28*
>
> *"All men are by nature equal, made all of the same earth by one Workman; and however we deceive ourselves, as dear unto God is the poor peasant as the mighty prince."*
> *~ Plato*

Maura, 42
Mother and Baby Girl

Giving birth should be one of the most joyous times of life and usually is. A newborn represents the very essence of life itself. The expectation of this event is like nothing else. Will it be a boy or a girl? Who will it look like? What are the parental visions for the child's future?...and on and on. It is most exciting for parents and all members of the extended family as well to think on these things. Sometimes, however, there can be unexpected devastating complications.

Maura was admitted for early labor. This was her fourth child, her fourth daughter, and the entire family was overjoyed to meet their new baby girl. Maura was ushered into delivery, with the baby being eight months along. After Maura delivered her, an unfortunate series of events occurred. Maura passed away right after delivery, never seeing her newborn.

My immediate thoughts and feelings were so inadequate, it was difficult for me to think that I might be of any comfort or help in any way, Here was this wonderful family ready to welcome their fourth child into the world with all their hopes and dreams and now experiencing life's ultimate defeat. While I'm aware of this being a common occurrence in impoverished and underdeveloped countries, I kept thinking, "how could this happen here?" We have the most advanced and most modern medical resources in the world. A heartbroken husband and three young daughters faced a most desperate and cruel time when there seemed to be no answers about why.

The family was understandably confused and hurt over losing Maura, yet quite naturally loving the baby girl with all their hearts. But why couldn't they have both, taking Maura home with the new baby girl like most families do? Any platitudes about faith, trust, and hope seemed to run out of steam. I felt unable to try to justify any aspect of this tragic occurrence.

I sat with them as they wept, holding a sweet, pink-cheeked baby girl in their arms. We sat in silence, in alternating emotions of pain and joy. As my thoughts rushed forth to where God is in these times, I immediately realized once again that "**I don't know where God is not**!" He is with us everywhere and always, available to give us His love and comfort in the most trying times when we need them most.

Maura's family will have her in their memories always, as four beautiful daughters live their lives with the legacy of a caring and loving mother.

> *"You will be secure, because there is hope; you will look about you and take your rest in safety."*
> *~ Job 11:18*
>
> *"What we have once enjoyed deeply we can never lose. All that we love deeply becomes a part of us."*
> *~ Helen Keller*

Nadine, 52
Pharmacist

Meeting new people and encountering new situations as we go through life are very much like the advice Forrest Gump received from his mother: "Life is like a box of chocolates. You never know what you're gonna get." This was never more true than when I first encountered Nadine. She had a scowl that penetrated all positive energy and laid waste to everything pleasant in the room. Anger emanated from her body, complete with clenched hands on the bedrails. I hesitated at the door as I saw her and must admit that I didn't feel at all confident about why I was there.

Her eyes immediately darted to the door and right at me. "What?" she yelled. "What do you want?"

As a young chaplain, I hadn't witnessed a lot of explosive situations. Quite honestly, I was unsure that going in was the best course of action for either of us. Still, I felt the pull to enter, so I stepped in. "Hi, I'm a chaplain here at the hospital. I was hoping we..." and before I could finish, she interrupted me. "I don't need a chaplain, Lady!" she yelled.

The bright yellow sunflower sky outside the window dramatically contrasted with her dark mood. I did my best to let a smile cross my face. "What are you looking at?" she asked, a bit calmed down .

"Well, Ms. Nadine, I was looking out the window at the beautiful sunshine, and now I'm looking at you. I was wondering if you'd like to talk for a few minutes," I said.

"Talk about what?" she grumbled. "There is nothing to talk about. Look at me. I can't move. I'm sick. I'm alone. My kids are in California. I have no one. I couldn't even get my purse when they called the ambulance. I don't have my things!" Instantly, I felt a swirl of empathy and sorrow for Nadine. I couldn't imagine having no loved ones nearby, and no access to my most personal belongings. I went into helper mode, wanting to collect her things from her apartment. Yet, that was out of bounds for what a chaplain was authorized to do in this situation. I promised her that I would inform her social worker that she wanted her purse.

"I'm so sorry you're going through all of this. It sounds very painful and hard," I said to her. Her face began to soften somewhat, her bottom lip now starting to quiver as she said, "I can't get any sleep here anyway, what with the nurses coming in every two hours. At least at my apartment I could sleep!" I nodded in understanding. "Yes, I know it's difficult to sleep here. Ms. Nadine…is there anything I can do for you?"

More than ever I now genuinely wanted to help her, somehow, some way. "Can you just please go get my purse?" she pleaded. I hesitated but said, "I'm not able to, but I will go right now and talk to your social worker. She can help with that." Nadine looked at me with a fresh expression of appreciation and said, "You would do that for me?" I stepped closer to her side, reaching my hand down and placed it on hers. "Ms. Nadine, I will help you in any way I can. I'm here just for you." Tears flowed down her pale cheeks. She held my hand firmly. "Will you promise to come back to see me?" she begged. I was thrilled to see that Nadine's anger and false sense of bravado were subsiding and that we now seemed to be connecting. "Yes, of course! I will see you again tomorrow," I told her.

I was thankful to learn later that her social worker orchestrated Nadine's purse delivery for which she was ecstatic and essentially calmed. With Nadine it was all too obvious just how important it is for all of us to have certain things, but, especially to have someone to hold onto. To help her through this crisis, I wanted desperately to be that someone for Nadine, while expressing to her that the most important "Someone," she could ever have is a loving God who has promised to walk with us through the darkest valleys and give us comfort, goodness, and love.

> *"Even youths will faint and be weary, and the young will fall exhausted; but those who wait for the Lord shall renew their strength, they shall mount up with wings like eagles, they shall run and not be weary, they shall walk and not faint."*
> *~ Isaiah 40:31*

> *"Hope is the thing with feathers, That perches in the soul, And sings the tune without the words, And never stops at all."*
> *~ Emily Dickinson*

Ted, 32
Banker

From a very young age, Ted had totally been into motorcycles. Around the age of ten he started riding dirt bikes and felt the thrill and fulfillment it gave him. It was the most exhilarating feeling he knew he would ever have. Worried about his safety when he turned sixteen, his parents got him a car, a sedan that they considered to be a safe mode of transportation. As time went on, however, he continued to be drawn to and interested in motorcycles. He referred to it as his "hobby" and often said riding made him "feel free." Ted would often say, "When I'm on a motorcycle, that's the time I'm the most me."

By the time he was twenty-one, he had saved enough money to buy a new bright blue Yamaha bike. He was extremely proud of the bike and proud that he had been able to buy it himself. His parents said there were many photos around the house of Ted and his prized possession.

Ted had a busy job in banking, but he spent any and every free moment riding. His favorite weekend activity was riding down the Natchez Trace Parkway, a scenic route that runs north-south 444 miles from Nashville, Tennessee to Natchez, Mississippi. Often, he would leave after work on Friday, then proceed down the Trace, thoroughly enjoying his feeling of freedom, as he took in the tranquil scenery with its greenery and tree-lined landscape. He would spend the nights at a roadside B&B, then make it back home to Nashville in time to return to work on Monday.

When I entered the trauma unit at the hospital, I saw multiple gurneys with unconscious patients, most heavily bandaged with severe bruising and bleeding and hooked up to constantly beeping lifesaving machines. I spotted a doctor speaking with a couple at a young man's side. As I approached, I was taken aback with the vision of this young man's physical condition. There was little of him to see that wasn't bruised or scraped or covered with bandages. He appeared to be in a horrific condition. When the doctor stepped away, I slowly approached the couple and introduced myself. Instantaneously, both fell into tears and sobs. Through the pain, they managed to reveal that their son, Ted, had been in a motorcycle accident. He had been on the interstate, riding safely and within the speed limit when a pickup struck him. He flipped and was tossed into a ravine. He was found unconscious about thirty feet from the blue Yamaha. A hospital helicopter had life-flighted him shortly after the wreck. His parents, who lived in another city, had gotten the first flight available and were now at his side. When they first saw him, his mom fainted and was placed on a gurney close by. Ted's dad expressed the hopeless feeing that he was losing both his son and his wife. Fortunately, she rebounded and revived within an hour and had returned to her son's side. She began to tell how the thing they feared most for Ted's life had come true.

Ted's terribly swollen eyes were sealed shut, deep in the realm of unconsciousness for three days. The doctor informed them that another brain scan would be done the next day in hopes of detecting meaningful activity. While the medical team remained hopeful, it was still very much touch and go.

I asked his parents if I might say a prayer for Ted. My request brought tears to both of them. I stood quietly for a moment, wondering if my request had somehow conveyed the wrong message that I felt Ted wasn't going to make it. I didn't want to invade their privacy, yet I didn't want to abandon them in this extreme and trying time. Ted's dad looked up, eyes in a sea of tears, and said, "Yes, would you pray for Ted?" I began offering thanks for a loving and merciful God, asking that He watch over Ted and bless him with His healing power. I prayed that Ted's parents would somehow be comforted and given peace, then faith for God's healing.

After about six weeks of hospitalization and rehab, Ted was discharged from the hospital. I was thankful and overjoyed to be able to follow him through his journey and see him wheeled out on a beautiful, sunny Friday. I'll always remember his thumbs up as the wheelchair carried him out to go home.

"I consider that the sufferings of this present time are not worth comparing with the glory about to be revealed to us."
~ Romans 8:18

"Although the world is full of suffering, it is also full of the overcoming of it."
~ Helen Keller

Flora, 70
Retired Bookkeeper

Flora was a client in a day unit for Alzheimer's patients. Her longterm memory was impeccable. She recalled her youth growing up in Germany with crystal detail. She repeated these same childhood stories in each conversation, approximately three times during each of our visits. Flora went into extensive retelling about her current home, the animals on the farm nearby whom she visited each afternoon, and the library in the nearby town. Flora knew so much, yet couldn't recall the day or time in the moment. If you encountered her in a social setting, you wouldn't know she had any health issues except when she mentioned the same story multiple times. She was physically fit, an expert at crossword puzzles, and loved to dance.

Someone once asked me, "Do you ever get tired of hearing the same stories, day in, day out?" While I can understand it might seem somewhat monotonous, I found it special and rewarding to listen as Flora was able to relive those moments each time she related a story. Especially so when her eyes brightened and her face lighted up while mentioning her pet cat, Lucy.

Portions of her childhood were difficult and seemed to be etched with some pain and discomfort, but she always spoke her truth with an infectious sincerity. And her love for her deceased husband, Estill! That love lived strongly inside her although he had been gone twenty years.

Flora's stories always touched me. No matter how many times she needed to tell them, it wasn't difficult to be completely captivated by her colorful sincerity. Never wavering, her eyes gleamed and her voice became strong whenever she spoke of her love for Estill. Even though this terrible and heartless disease affected her so cruelly, the power of love persisted strongly within her.

> *"For I am convinced that neither death nor life, neither angels nor demons, neither height nor depth, nor anything else in all creation, will be able to separate us from the love of God that is in Christ Jesus our Lord."*
> *~ Romans 8:38-39*
>
> *"Always, everywhere God is present, and always He seeks to discover himself to each one."*
> *~ A.W. Tozer*

Meaghan, 29
Mother

She was as still as a glass figurine. Her eyes were closed like envelopes. Meaghan was not in pain. She was young, much too young to be facing the end of her life to cancer. Her two wide-eyed toddlers were squirming in the arms of her husband who was trying to be the attentive and doting father as if she would wake soon from a nap. But his hands were truly full as he looked at her knowing that Meaghan was passing from this world.

The weighted stillness in the air was in direct contrast to the certain peace on Meaghan's face. The overwhelming and sad feelings her husband was now experiencing represented one of life's ultimate and unfortunate but familiar conflicts. Wanting her to stay yet wanting her to no longer suffer the pain that filled her life was heartwrenching. How could someone so young, so full of life be leaving, but not on her own terms? Now, she was leaving two typically active and loving children and a husband who was having to envision life with a totally different outcome. Fairness was not in the equation here. Everyone earnestly hoped for healing for Meaghan. Her church family had prayed incessantly for three years. Yet her healing was to come only in the form of rest and peace beyond this earth.

I spoke the most difficult prayer ever. The gut punch I felt to utter words that might usher Meaghan into the afterlife was something I'll never forget. Her little children were losing their mother, and her husband was losing his wife. I prayed fervently for her healing, but also for peace and comfort for her family and friends. Holding onto faith at this moment was like dangling from a bridge with one finger, while posing the ultimate question: Why? Yet in these times of darkness the spirit of God is abiding if we open our hearts and minds and try to see the light, however faint it might seem at first. Our struggles can draw us closer to God and deepen our trust in Him.

> *"Trust in the Lord with all your heart and lean not on your own understanding."*
> *~ Proverbs 3:5*

> *"Hope is being able to see that there is light despite all of the darkness."*
> *~ Desmond Tutu*

Marie, 82
Mother

Marie was struggling to reach the straw to her drink as I entered her room. "Dear, can you help me?" she asked.

I went to her side to assist with her water. "Sure, I'm happy to," I answered as I gently guided the straw to her parched lips, still remembering the sight of her hands, shaking and incapable of performing this basic function. After she swallowed, she appreciatively remarked, "Thank you. You're a nice nurse."

I replied, "No, Ma'am, actually I'm a chaplain here at the hospital." She looked confused with this information. "The doctor?" she asked. "No, I'm a chaplain. I wanted to visit with you and see if you would like to talk awhile."

She looked off in deep thought, straining hard to understand. "I'm not sure what you're saying," she said.

I wanted her to know I was someone who had come to see her, simply to visit and just listen if she wanted to talk. Titles or names didn't matter. "Ms. Marie, I thought maybe we could talk for a little bit."

At this suggestion, her demeanor changed. She lit up like the brightest firefly on a summer night. "Oh...I know! You're here for the trip today! Let me get my things," she exclaimed as she pointed at a chair with two plastic bags. The bags were stuffed full of her personal belongings, clothes, shoes, and toiletry items. She was obviously very frail and bedridden and could hardly move, but she was now attempting to exit the bed. Just then an alarm sounded in the room. "BEEP, BEEP,

BEEP," was repeated in a sequence of threes. Two nurses ran in. "Ms. Marie! You can't leave your bed," they said.

Marie was instantaneously very angry. "Aw turn the damn thing off!" she yelled. The happy, childlike Marie had morphed into a very defiant and outraged patient. "You can't keep telling me what to do!" she yelled at them. Then she pointed at me. "She's here to take me on the trip today." I looked at the nurses, unsure of just how to respond to this increasingly volatile scene, and the suggestion that I might be taking her on a trip.

"What trip is that, Ms. Marie?" one nurse asked.

"You tell them," she said to me.

In a somewhat soft and solicitous tone, I said, "Ms. Marie, I'm not exactly sure what trip you're referring to," while tenderly resting my hand in a reassuring gesture on her shoulder.

She squinted and whispered, "Honey, you know. Rhode Island. Remember, dear?" The nurses had disabled the alarm and were shuffling out.

In an effort to further calm her and engage her in conversation, I asked, "Ms. Marie, tell me about Rhode Island." She smiled again, returning to the happy woman I'd met earlier. "Well, when the bus arrives, you and I will go to Rhode Island. We will go to my niece's house on the water. We will drink tea and have such a grand time! Oh, my...I can't wait to take this trip with you."

Her demeanor, now so sweet and her plans to include me, even in such an unrealistic scenario, created a lot of uncertainty as to how I should proceed. I desperately wanted to comfort her and be her friend, but I knew that abruptly telling her the trip wasn't happening would cause her pain and could only create more upsetting dynamics. We sat in silence a few minutes.

The birds were performing a symphony in the trees outside the window. Marie drifted off to sleep, clinging to her sheet, her frail hands at rest. I rose, adjusted her bedding, and calmly said, "Ms. Marie, I'll be back tomorrow to see you," all the while thanking God for comfort and peace, and well-being for Ms. Marie. She continued her sleep. I hoped and prayed that maybe she was dreaming of drinking tea in Rhode Island. Maybe it could all come true as she dreamed.

> *"Come to me, all you that are weary and are carrying heavy burdens, and I will give you rest."*
> *~ Matthew 11:28*
>
> *"Why did you do all this for me?" he asked. "I don't deserve it. I've never done anything for you."*
> *"You have been my friend," replied Charlotte. "That in itself is a tremendous thing."*
> *~ E.B. White*

Carol, 49
Real Estate Agent

Carol was sitting in a chair looking out the window at a somewhat dismal and foggy day with her bandaged leg propped upon the bed. I knocked, asking if I might come in to visit with her.

"Who are you, a social worker or something?" she inquired. After I replied that I was the chaplain, she shook her head no, explaining, "No thank you, I'm an atheist."

Working as an interfaith chaplain means I must also respect and communicate with non-believers. I nodded in understanding and said, "Okay, I hear you. Just let me know if you change your mind about visiting. I'm not here to preach," I said with a little wink. At this, she seemed to warm up and smiled a bit. It was as if my acceptance of her declaration of not believing in God and my promise of no evangelizing swayed her. She then invited me, waving me in as if we were longtime friends.

"I just don't believe in God," she began. "If you knew the things I've been through in life..." She hesitated and her gaze went back to the window. "I lost my parents in a wreck when I was a little girl, just six years old. Then I went to live with my aunt, and she got breast cancer and died when I was nine. After that it was foster care." It was obvious that she had experienced extreme loss and pain.

As I sat with her in that wounded space, she suddenly asked, "What about you, Chaplain?" I was caught off guard a bit and was immediately tempted to respond and share with her that I, too, had experienced great loss that had affected my life in many significant ways.

"Yes, Carol," I replied, while taking a few seconds to clear my thoughts. "I have carried heavy loss and grief as well…still do." But I knew this was her time and hoped this would be an opening to establish a meaningful dialogue that might prove to be helpful.

Then the big question came: "Chaplain, how does a person still believe in God when they've experienced so much hurt in this life? Why would God allow so much bad to happen, shattering our lives in ways that cause us to lose all hope?"

I gathered my thoughts, took a deep breath, then said, "I have absolutely no idea why bad things happen and why life can be filled at times with overwhelming pain and grief. I just don't have good answers for that. But alongside the pain I carry, I carry God alongside me, too. I know He is standing with me so I'm never alone. As I seek His comfort, love, and grace, He fills my life with joy and gives me strength to carry on."

She turned her head to the side, and it became obvious that she was having very deep thoughts. "I want that," she quietly and surprisingly said, as she looked at me, her eyes glistening ever so slightly. "I want to feel that God is with me …giving me comfort and helping me to find peace and joy." In that moment, a prayer was lifted up to lead Carol to open her heart and mind to a belief in God and a walk of faith that might provide her with newfound strength and joy. We continued talking for a few more minutes, then her nurse arrived.

As I left her room, I couldn't be positive what impact our conversation had on Carol, but I truly felt there had been an awakening within her as she expressed a desire to seek God and to want the peace and comfort that can come from Him. I hope she always remembers she is never alone.

"When you go through deep waters, I will be with you."
~ Isaiah 43:2

"You never really understand a person until you consider things from his point of view...Until you climb inside of his skin and walk around in it."
~ **Harper Lee,** *To Kill a Mockingbird*

Sarah, 85
Retired Government Employee

Sarah fumbled with her fork, poking at a typical hospital food concoction, expressing some hesitation about eating it. She had crumbs on her chin and on the front of her gown. Her shaky hand was doing its best to transport a bite from the tray to her mouth...clearly a struggle. When I walked in to visit, she was welcoming and warm. She shoved the tray away in slight disgust and invited me to sit down.

"Well, well, so you're the chaplain. I saw the priest earlier. He was wonderful!" She furrowed her brow in an attempt to read my ID tag. "What is your denomination?" she asked. I explained to her that I was an interfaith chaplain, meaning I serve all faiths, or no faith at all. I am an equal opportunity listener, for anyone at anytime. She looked at me cynically like this was maybe too good to be true, like I had a different truth up my sleeve. I wasn't offended. Many people have trouble trusting random clergy who wander into their room.

She soon cast aside her doubts and opened up to me about her life (we call it "life review" in chaplain circles). She had lost her husband twenty years earlier. She had three grown children, seven grandchildren, and two great-grandchildren on the way. After a few moments of conversation, she glanced out the window on a sunny horizon and poignantly revealed, "I've had a good life." Then she turned to me as if in a lightbulb moment and said, "You know the priest was really good. So are you. You got a gift." Tearing up somewhat at these heartwarming words I thanked her from deep within my heart. Once again, a valuable lesson was mine to learn and one that I was learning on a daily basis: In these moments of attempting to bring love, comfort, and cheer, the intended recipients often give us more than we could ever give them.

I was reminded of Matthew 18:20, "For where two or three gather in my name, there am I with them." I felt that Sarah and I had surely done that.

> *"...remembering the words of the Lord Jesus, for he himself said, 'It is more blessed to give than to receive.'"*
> *~ Acts 20:35*
>
> *"You can give without loving, but you can never love without giving."*
> *~ Robert Louis Stevenson*

Malik, 26
Store Manager

When I first met Malik, he was preparing to undergo his first chemotherapy treatment. He lived three hours away, which under more normal circumstances might be viewed sometimes as nothing more than a casual drive into the city. But these weren't "normal circumstances." They not only posed a life-changing challenge for Malik but they created an emotional upheaval within his family by his having to leave them to face such a dire and totally unknown outcome.

Malik was alone and very lonely. A chaplain had been referred to Malik by his nurse and at his request. He was lying back, head propped at forty-five degrees, face gleaming with a large, welcoming smile. An IV machine just to his right pumped in what was hoped to be a cancer-killing solution. The gray winter day outside the window cast long shadows on his hospital wall.

I gently and somewhat hesitantly approached his bedside, ready to listen and desperately wanting to be both comforting and understanding. Quickly, the radiant smile disappeared, turning into a quiver. The tears flowed easily and in abundance. My heart was deeply touched and for a few seconds I was speechless. "Hi, Malik, I'm the chaplain here, and I would like to visit with you. Would you like to talk?" His eyes slowly turned downward.

"So much has happened to him..." I heard a voice from the corner. I turned to see an older woman. Her hair was neatly up in a bun, and she wore tortoise-shell glasses. "I'm his mother, Elzie. Malik has had a real tough go of it." As she continued to describe his circumstances, her comments so filled with love and expressing understanding, his sobbing ceased. He looked longingly at her, and her facial expression conveyed what only a mother's can.

"Malik, I want you to know I am here for you in this moment. How can I help? May I pray with you?"

Malik revealed, "I have multiple myeloma. Today is my first day of chemo...I'm very scared." At this very moment after revealing his fear, the most loving demeanor and beautiful smile graced his face, and with uplifted eyes, he said, "I do believe God is somewhere out there." At this revelation of his belief, Elzie quickly moved to his side and said, "Malik, God is right here with us. Right now." Elzie took his hand, and as they looked into each other's eyes, you could see the love they felt for each other and a peace from sharing their belief that God "is with us right now."

> *"So we have come to know and to believe the love that God has for us. God is love, and whoever abides in love abides in God, and God abides in him."*
> *~ 1 John 4:16*
>
> *"Never be afraid to trust an unknown future to a known God."*
> *~ Corrie ten Boom*

TONY, 42
Unemployed

I was visiting with a cardiac patient when the pager began to buzz. I excused myself and when I saw where the page was from, I braced myself for the unknown. I had never visited this particular unit before. Rooms there were separated by glass and curtains, much more private and very spacious for equipment.

I asked the charge nurse for more information on Tony, the patient I was there to see. He was suffering from schizophrenia, emphysema, pneumonia, and liver disease. Additionally, he was in restraints due to combative behavior. In the most recent outburst, he had asked to see a priest. He felt his time of death was near. I felt anxious as she described what could only be an unpredictable scenario.

The nurse said, "The doors are open, and we will stand right outside the door as backup for you." Needing backup was not something I had prepared for in my chaplaincy studies. Yet, in my role and commitment to serve others, I knew and felt I needed to be responsive to anyone in need, including Tony. With that in mind I proceeded to do my best to live up to and fulfill my promise to help others.

Slowly, I turned to the second door where he was. A white curtain covered the open doorway. I felt my hands growing clammy. I reached for the curtain, leaning my head in where I could now see Tony. His arms and legs were strapped to the bed. A security officer was seated on the far side of the room. Tony's eyes were full of fire. I stepped into the room, maintaining a safe distance at the foot of the bed. "Hi, Tony. I'm the chaplain here. You wanted to speak with someone?" I asked.

This infuriated him. "Hey, little girl, you ain't no priest!" The officer spoke up, "Calm down, Tony. You remember what happened last time." Tony was visibly shaking, quaking beneath the restraints. "I'm gonna die. I'm gonna die! I need last rites from a priest!" he screamed. The officer stood up, walking toward the bed. Tony was suffering so badly. I could feel his hurt. "Okay, Tony. I can page the priest for you," I said in a calm voice. "Come here, girl," he implored. He was trying to reach his hands up beneath the straps. His eyes were still fiery and full of rage.

I stepped over to his side. "I know you want a priest, and I understand. Would you like for me to pray with you now?" I asked.

He looked away, drool rolling down the corner of his mouth. He went silent. I remained in place, awaiting his answer. There is a fine line with patients many times. A chaplain wants to be there for them, but not if he or she is not wanted. Respecting the patient's decision is paramount. It may be the only space in their time of hospitalization where they can make a decision for themselves. Such was the case with Tony.

After what seemed like an eternity, he returned his gaze and looked up at me. "Okay," he said reluctantly. I placed my hand on his left hand. Feeling his tension, I covered his hand with a tranquil palm. I spoke a prayer for Tony to receive peace in his heart and calm in his soul.

These words seemed to soothe him and he looked up at me, his face now expressing a softness of understanding and much-needed serenity. The change in his demeanor was astounding. It was obvious that God's peace and comfort surpass all.

"For the LORD your God is living among you. He is a mighty savior. He will take delight in you with gladness. With his love, he will calm all your fears. He will rejoice over you with joyful songs."
~ Zephaniah 3:17

"Did I offer peace today? Did I bring a smile to someone's face? Did I say words of healing? Did I let go of my anger and resentment? Did I forgive? Did I love? These are the real questions. I must trust that the little bit of love that I sow now will bear many fruits, here in this world and the life to come."
~ Henri Nouwen

Tony

Lula, 66
Retired Schoolteacher

Lula was a small, near child-sized figure snuggled under several white blankets. The room was lowly lit and spartanly uncluttered. A series of muted beeps echoed from the machine beside her. I slipped in with as little fanfare as possible and tried my best to quietly assess the situation. But Lula's head quickly jerked to the left, and her eyes immediately honed in on me. Looking inquisitively, her face was filled with questions. Once I explained to her who I was, she was more than ready and quite eager to talk. I told her that I was a chaplain and hoped that our visit and conversation might help her feel better.

Lula shifted in her bed, leaning up to see me more clearly. "Tell me," she implored, "tell me why I'm going through this pain, this illness. Since you're a chaplain, you must know. Why do bad things happen to good people?"

I was immediately taken aback by the impact of this overwhelming, yet well-known question, but I did my best to stay in the moment with her. Attempting to not be distracted by my own emotional reactions, I momentarily hesitated and then said, "Lula, why many things happen in life the way they do is not something we can always know or fully understand." Not liking my answer, in a somewhat challenging manner, she said, "So you're saying you don't know? You don't know why some people overcome serious illness and near death, while others don't?"

I looked at her with anguish in my heart, feeling momentarily and grossly inadequate. With love and sincerity, I simply said, "No...I don't know." Lula retorted with a chuckle, "Well, can you go find someone who does know? Is there anyone here who knows?"

I reached over, placing my hand on hers. "Lula," I said, "Comfort comes from a healing God...believing in Him and having faith in things we cannot see." Lula faintly smiled.

> *"Now faith is confidence in what we hope for and assurance about what we do not see."*
> *~ Hebrews 11:1*
>
> *"All I have seen teaches me to trust the creator for all I have not seen."*
> *~ Ralph Waldo Emerson*

John and Kathleen, 33 & 31
Media Consultant and Nurse

The joy of anticipation in a family planning the birth of a child has no equal as there are so many thoughts, dreams, and plans that surround this blessed event. With all the preparations that are necessary, there is little time or space for anything else. The fun of preparing the nursery space and being sure all necessary supplies are in place begin to firm up the reality that for sure, this event is on its way. The overwhelming feeling an expectant parent gets when looking forward to holding, cradling and loving the child can be completely consuming.

A call was received in our pastoral care office to visit a room on the maternity floor. It was an area I had long desired to see, and I was looking forward to going. When I entered the room, I saw a man gathering items and carefully placing them in a duffle bag. He turned and said, "Oh hi, Kathleen is in the bathroom. She'll be right out."

Suddenly, his half-smile disappeared and was replaced with a look of pain and sorrow. "It's been really tough," he said, tears now slowly beginning to well up. Kathleen emerged, and she too teared up as soon as our eyes met. "Hi, I heard you wanted to see a chaplain?" This was all I could think of to say at the moment, hoping that this might open the door to our conversation and interaction.

Both John and Kathleen immediately broke down in streaming tears and obvious flowing heartache. Their first baby, a boy they'd named Joshua, had just died at seven months gestation. The doctors had hope for him early on soon after he was born, but his body just wasn't developed enough to sustain life outside that of his mother's. He passed hours later. I immediately and strongly identified with this pain, almost like I was transported into their personal anguish. I had suffered miscarriages and although my babies hadn't grown to seven months, I knew the feeling and sense of loss and disappointment of expectation. I knew the feeling of going from elation to despair. I also knew how badly John and Kathleen wanted Joshua to live and could imagine the anxiety, stress, and devastation they must have gone through during this critical time of hoping and praying for the best. I asked if there was anything I could do or any way I could help. They simultaneously answered, "Prayer." We held hands in a small circle, praying through streams of salty tears of unfathomable sadness. I asked God for peace for John and Kathleen, acknowledging that while we didn't understand why Joshua did not live, so much is beyond our comprehension and understanding. Staying rooted in the soil of trust and faith is crucial while continuing to look to God for comfort and compassion. We prayed that John and Kathleen would seek and find this.

> *"And the peace of God, which surpasses all understanding, will guard your hearts and your minds in Christ Jesus."*
> *~ Philippians 4:7*
>
> *"If you believe in God, He will open the windows of heaven and pour blessings upon you."*
> *~ Mahalia Jackson*

From the author...

In times of personal crises everyone needs comfort, love, and support, no matter the nature of the crisis. Whether physical, emotional, or a case of being overwhelmed by life's circumstances, nothing is more comforting during these times than to feel that there is someone who cares. A specific personal crisis is unfortunately not a single dimensional dilemma but is usually compounded by invading other areas of one's life.

A serious or life-threatening medical condition can lead to extreme emotional instability as well, impacting not only the person who is experiencing and going through this, but other family members also. This is where the importance of care, love, and comfort play such an important role. After interacting and communicating with so many who faced such dire circumstances, this was undoubtedly the case. Their willingness and inclination to express this importance was both heart warming and ultimately very revealing.

With rare exception, a strong belief in God brought peace and calm to both patient and family members as they dealt with their crises. Prayer was always forthcoming and comforting, and provided apparent hope for healing and recovery. In times of sorrow and discouragement, looking to God with faith and belief in His mercies and understanding was the defining conclusion, believing that God is Someone who cares....

> "Blessed be the God and Father of our Lord Jesus Christ, the Father of mercies and God of all comfort, who comforts us in all our tribulation, that we may be able to comfort those who are in any trouble, with the comfort with which we ourselves are comforted by God."
> ~ II Corinthians 1: 3-4

Notes...

...Have you experienced a time in your life when you felt absolutely alone, as if God was totally absent?

_____
_____
_____
_____
_____
_____
_____
_____
_____

...Has there been a time in your life when you fully felt and sensed God's presence?

_____
_____
_____
_____
_____
_____
_____
_____
_____

Notes...

...What are your personal beliefs regarding God's presence in your life and in the world today?

_____
_____
_____
_____
_____
_____
_____
_____

...If you could ask God three questions, what would they be?

_____
_____
_____
_____
_____
_____
_____
_____